The Honey Sutras

Soul Wisdom

from the birds and the bees

by Ingrid Goff-Maidoff

ISBN 978-1-886631-04-5

Sarah's Circle Publishing
Martha's Vineyard
21 Marion's Way
Chilmark, MA 02535 USA
www.TendingJoy.com

For Rose and Bella

and all daughters everywhere.

Honey Musings and an Introduction

When I add a spoon of honey to my tea, I give thanks to a dozen bees for the work of their whole lives. When my finger sweeps the final drop of sweetness from the jar, I know we've enjoyed the nectar from over a million flowers. This is what honey is: the souls of flowers, a food to please the gods. Honeyeaters know that to have a joyful heart one must live life like the bees, sipping the sweet nectar from each moment as it blooms. And Life, like the world of honey, has its enchantments and its stings. We learn to mingle caution with desire. Yet a beekeeper might tell us that the first sting hurts the most. We grow thicker skinned, respectful, unafraid. And the heart that becomes bitter is the one that counts the stings....

I wrote this book when my two daughters would soon be curious about the birds and the bees, and I anticipated having the usual talks. But what I most wanted to speak to them of was their internal radiance, and why they are worthy of the utmost kindness, respect, and love. I wanted to tell them how beautiful they are, how splendid life is, and what a contribution a spiritual practice can be to finding happiness, harmony and purpose. It was my hope that once they knew the boundless depths of their hearts, they could experience love from a place of fullness, worthiness, friendship and joy. I am so pleased that these words have resonated with so many yoga and meditation practitioners as well.

The Honey Sutras are comprised of "stitches in consciousness"~ meditations and short sayings which speak to the blossoming of the heart. Each selection bears witness to the fragrance of the sacred realm within us all, a realm of eternal love, infinite beauty, divine wisdom and radiant energy. These passages intend to plant the seeds of a sweet life philosophy, in hopes that the reader will learn to identify with love first, and not little fears or feelings of inadequacy. The soul is her base, the personality is second.

Each selection in the Honey Sutras is an invitation for deeper reflection. Learning the practice of centering into love through stillness and reflection is at the heart of the message of this book. In the words of Saint Teresa of Avila, "As soon as you apply yourself to reflection, you will feel at once your senses gather themselves together; they seem like bees which return to the hive and there shut themselves up to work at the making of honey."

These words are the result of many years exploring the world's spiritual traditions to gather wisdom and beauty~ the way the bee gathers nectar, or an anthologist gathers flowers. The end-notes provide information for further reading, and any original texts that I adapted, or set out from, in an effort to maintain the poetic voice of the Sutras.

Peace and Love,

~Ingrid Goff-Maidoff

How could the soul not take flight
when from the glorious Presence
A soft calling flows sweet as honey,
Comes right up to her and whispers,
"Rise up now, come away."
~Rumi

Observing all with a loving eye,
let your spirit expand outward,
soaring as the dove above the
round globe of the earth...
Look upon its mountains,
forests, fields, and rivers,
rich expanses of wilderness,
cities and village squares...
Gaze upon its moonlit lakes,
its gardens and its oceans.
Now taking yourself further still,
move beyond the stars in the sky.

Remembering all you have seen,
you hold in your mind the Universe.
Now, turning this universe outside in,
feel it unfolding gently inside you,
opening layer by layer
like a many petalled flower.
This is your innerverse,
the landscape of your soul.
It is the heart you are invited to explore.

鷽 垂櫻

Before sharing your heart with another,
you must travel its many lands.
Absorb the fragrance of its gardens,
gaze up at its vast, star glittered skies,
drink deeply from its rivers,
listen to its music,
dream a portion of its dreams,
and rest upon its shores.

Honey Sutras begin with the heart.
To know one's heart
is to know boundless love.

You are the wind, the ocean,

the moonlit lake...

You are the sun, the blue iris, the bee.

You are the rain and the green fields.

You are the sparrow and the

sparrow's song.

You are the apple tree and its blossoms.

You are the nest in the branch of the tree.

You are the speckled egg in the nest,

and the gentle body keeping it warm.

You are the honey in the honeycomb,
the hive and the working bee.
You are the flower, the pollen,
the nectar.
You are the golden candle
and its flame.

You hold every joy, every sadness,
all that has been and will be...

The world hums a secret music:
the melodies of birds,
the language of the bees,
the breath of the wind,
the murmur of the ocean...
everything around you sings.

Even at a tender age,
you have had glimpses
of your own divine radiance.

There is honey inside you,
the honey of the divine.
It is in everybody and everything.
One taste of this sweetness
changes your life forever.

但使姚家
鎮長在
洛陽亭畔不凡塵

廣重筆

You will know joy
when you love your Self.
What is this Self?
It is the ocean you are melted in.

~

More than your character, habits,
or needs, more than the voice that
chatters like a scolding squirrel
high in a tree,
your Self is the Divine light within you.
It is your essence ~
the deep consciousness
that knows peace, love,
and compassionate understanding.

Self knows its own sweetness.
Self lights its own way.
Self needs nothing,
living in contentment,
fullness, harmony and joy.

Consider the phrase:
Be true to yourself.
Now reflect upon its meaning...

Self holds you in an eternal embrace,
and you hold Self
like a hidden treasure.
Love this Self as Self loves you,
and a light will glow from your heart,
your eyes, your words, your deeds.

The Upanishads say:
This Self is the
Honey of all beings,
and all beings are
the Honey of this Self.

Other sacred names for Self are:

Divine Wisdom, Consciousness, Presence,
God, Peace, Love, Soul, Radiance, Goodness,
Goddess, Allah, Brahma, Oneness,
The One, Wakantanka, Jehova, The Tao,
The Divine, Joy, The Infinite, Wholeness,
The Holy, Fullness, Beloved Luminous
Essence, The Ground of All Being...

Which name do you find
the sweetest on your tongue?
Never hesitate to address
that name in song and prayer.

Before you can love another wholly,
you yourself must become whole.
The path to wholeness
sees the Holy in all things.

Possessing ultra-violet vision,
honeybees see through flowers
to detect their hidden nectar.
When we develop similar vision,
we see the nectar inside others.

Within everyone there is gold,
there is an interior world
to be explored,
and there is something
to cherish and to love.

When a friend says, "Namaste,"
they are saying, "The Divine in me
salutes the Divine in you."
When Jesus said,
"The kingdom of God is within you,"
this is what he meant.

NAMASTE

I honor the place in you
in which the entire universe dwells.
I honor the place in you
which is of love, of truth,
of light and of peace.
When you are in that place in you,
and I am in that place in me,
we are one.

Honor the place in yourself
in which the entire universe dwells.
This is the landscape of your heart,
the growing flower
of your consciousness ~
ever expanding, timeless,
without limit, without end.

When you honor the Self
in all beings
throughout the natural world,
you grow in understanding
that all are intertwined.
The relation of your soul
with the World Soul
becomes a splendid love affair.

花下忘帰因美景
樽前勧酔是春風
廣重筆

Voices of distraction
want to fill you
with a sense of need.
Urging you to
purchase every product,
their motivation is greed.

When you remember
the treasure in your heart,
there is nothing whatsoever
that you need to buy.

Remember who you are.
Know that you are loved.
Rest. Be at peace.
In the arms of the Divine
you become yourself.

Never let anyone convince you
that you are anything less
than a miracle.
You are part of the Whole,
an expression of Supreme Love.

Always

always

return to love.

~

Returning to love,
you are like a bird that has
left a dark cage,
spreading her joyful wings
to travel the infinite sky.

Practice kindness and your world
becomes a prospering garden.
Practice kindness and return
to love's embrace.

Bees spend their lives making honey.
People make honey
through their acts of peace and love.

Practice compassionate presence
toward all others, and yourself.
Learn to be a gentle friend
to the love within all beings.
Once mindful compassion is realized,
a light lights in the soul.
A warm passion and peace enfold you,
and an interior radiance glows.
The heart becomes generous,
the tongue becomes sweet,
the mind supple and forgiving.

You are like a flower,
perfuming the air with your fragrance.
You are a bird
singing the song in your heart.
You are the honeybee
making honey with your life.

You have a heart that flows with honey,
a soul the essence of nectar,
and the pollen of good ideas
to help bring peace to this world.

Learn to see the world
through the eyes of the heart,

Luminous clarity!

Learn to listen
with the ears of the heart~

Marvelous music!

Arise my love, my beautiful one,
and turn from your forgetting.
There is wisdom
you have the treasure of
that sometimes needs reminding:

It is true: beneath all things,
you are beautiful,
you are loved,
you are here for a purpose.

To be beautiful is to remember
you are already full of beauty:
Closing your eyes,
bring light into your heart.
Think of your whole being
as a cup to fill,
or a lamp to be lit.
Imagine yourself filling
with joyful peace, God, love, light,
sweetness, honey radiance.
This is the source of beauty.
When there is light in the soul,
there is beauty in the person.

The Chinese have a proverb,
and its words are these:

When there is light in the soul,
there is beauty in the person.
When there is beauty in the person,
there is harmony in the home.
When there is harmony in the home,
there is honor in the nation.
When there is honor in the nation,
there can be peace in the world.

When you light a candle,
remember the light in your soul.
Reflect on this blessing of Jesus:
You are the Light of the World.

~

In silent meditation,
turn your inner eye
toward the light.

翡翠
鳶尾艸 瞿麦

Divine energy courses through you,
works through you,
sings, plays, and creates through you ~
exuberant like the honeybee
carrying pollen from flower to flower.

The honeybee practices alchemy,
transforming nectar into liquid gold.
You too may practice such alchemy,
through your thoughts, your deeds,
even with your breath.

Do not overlook the breath.
So many take for granted
this essential gift of life.

In the morning when you awake,
breathe in peace, breathe out love.
At the market, on the street,
breathe in peace, breathe out love.
Among friends and even strangers,
breathe in peace, breathe out love.

As your day progresses, you may
choose different breathing meditations:

In the afternoon, walking or sitting,
breathe in love, breathe out joy.
In the evening before retiring,
breathe in joy, breathe out thanks.

名所江戸百景

Develop the practices of stillness,
meditation, reflection, prayer.
You will discover
that this is a great gift.
Treasure this practice.
It is of more value
than any earthly jewel.

Contemplation means
to enter the temple in your heart.
By taking refuge in stillness,
balance may be restored,
confidence, energy,
peace and love.

Returning to the heart,
listening to the stillness,
you bloom like a rose
growing near a spring-fed stream.

Send out your sweet fragrance
like the petals of a lily.
Sing your songs of wonder
like the nightingale at dawn.

Center yourself in silence.
Dropping your cloak of worries,
empty the mind of doubt, fear,
and other feelings of despair.
Sitting in stillness,
feel the Universe flow
sweetly back in.
Love will come
like an ocean tide to an empty cove.
You will be blessed with radiant peace.
This is the essence of you.

Sometimes we must empty the mind
in order to let the Universe in.

Sitting in stillness,
you are like a plum tree growing
on the banks of a deep river.
Reach your roots through the earth
into the water to drink.
The river is sacred spirit.
When you stay connected
you do not feel thirst,
your blossoms grow fragrant
and you produce sweet fruit.

Some call it
the land of milk and honey.
Some call it the kingdom of God.
For others, it is perfect peace,
infinite knowing,
The Ground of Being,
the land of the heart,
a garden paradise.

In silence and in stillness
Sacred Spirit brings you there.

Love's kiss tastes of honey,
drenching us with its sweetness.
The heart opens, unfolding,
like a million petalled flower.

The day will come
when you meet another
whose soulful kiss
is delicious to you.
They will appear to you
like an apple tree among
the trees of the woods.
You will shine for them
like a lily among the brambles.

Your heart will swell and sing
like the Robin courting the dawn.
your thoughts will start to drift
like milkweed on the wind.
You may feel drunk like the bird
who's eaten berries turned to wine.
Your world will expand with music,
merriment and laughter.
Your body will want to dance and play,
spreading its newfound wings.
You may costume yourself like a flower,
applying alluring fragrance,
in hopes to enchant their eyes, their lips,
and later to win their heart.

All long to be seen
through the tender eyes of love.
All long to be touched
by the tender hands of love.
All long to be heard
with the tender ears of love.

The eyes and hands
and ears of love
know the body is a temple,
the mind a sanctuary of wisdom,
and the soul a sacred realm
from which each of us has emerged.

A lover will want to roam with you
the landscape of your heart,
and, taking your hand, invite you
to venture into theirs.

Love is the meeting of souls,
world within world unfolding.
Heart to heart,
each door opens to the other.
Gardens of memory, passion,
and dreams pour through.
A new world emerges
to share and to explore.

True love knows
your heart is blossoming,
to reveal the treasure within you.
True love longs to hear the song
your heart was born to sing.
True love tastes the honey.
True love sees the light.

Every moment with each other
is a moment to be kind.
Every gesture, every word,
is a messenger of love.
Every day you spend together,
be mindful of its blessings.
Turn your heart to the sacred,
the sacred is always there.

Honeyeaters know life has
its sweetness and its stings.
Touching the rose,
one risks the prick of thorns.
Lighting a candle flame
could burn down a whole house.
Giving one's heart too soon
might risk a fickle lover.

A lover must wait
at their darling's door,
never forcing entrance
into her sacred realm.
When the heart's door opens willingly,
a garden of love is revealed.
If the door is forced from the outside,
there will be a land darkened with fear.

Keep your body safe.
Don't be afraid to sting.

True love is gentle, honest,
patient, and kind.
True love creates a mutual world.
True love expands the lover.
True love will never diminish another.

Do not cling to suffering, making it your way
of being in the world. Do not repeat,
"Oh, how I've been stung," hiding yourself
in a room of darkness and despair.
Become wiser, more courageous.
No-one said this would be easy.

To say roses shouldn't have thorns
would rob their fragrance of its power.
To say candles shouldn't burn
would snuff out their luminous light.
Insist that honeybees should not sting,
and all rewards would be less sweet.
Avoiding love, your soul will wither,
like a garden parched by drought.

Sometimes tears are the rain
your garden needs to grow.

Life becomes as we are,
often reflecting our own nature,
fulfilling our expectations:
the bitter and the sweet.

A bee does not bring bitter nectar
back into the hive.
Be aware of what you take
into your body and your mind.

Gather wisdom
as the bee gathers nectar:
go from flower to flower,
finding teachings everywhere.
Bring what you learn
to the rich honeycomb
of your mind.

Birds sing in summer's branches
trusting their needs will be met,
yet have the wisdom to move on
when the landscape no longer provides.
Have trust and heed the seasons.
If you are called to spread your wings,
do not remain out of habit
in a forest that cannot sustain you.
Do not keep the dwelling
of your body,
your heart,
or your mind
in a place that does not nourish
a healthy and happy life.

The nectar from more than
a million flowers
comprise a pound of honey.
The worker bee contributes
only a drop or two on her own.

Greater results are often seen
when efforts are combined.
Each community is like a hive
supported by working bees.

Live well, savoring your moments
like honey on your tongue.
Let your life absorb the fragrance
of the garden that is love.

Fill your cup of gratitude
all the way to the brim.
When your cup overflows,
the spirit lifts,
and love emanates
a peaceful joy
throughout your whole being.

Gather nectar from
the sweetest flowers:
silent meditation,
time in nature,
art, music, poetry,
the company of
family and friends.

Be mindful of your speech:
avoid using words that sting.

Concentrate on gratitude,
creativity and forgiveness.
Keeping your mind positive,
consider all that you love.
Remember all that you are
thankful for,
and all that you can give.
Remain an open vessel,
allowing love to flow through you.
Give as much as you can
with your generous,
compassionate heart.

As the bee sips nectar
without harming the flower,
walk lightly in this world
taking no more than you need.

Something that slumbered
inside you stirs,
as if awakening from a dream.
Do you hear the distant music?
It is your heart beginning to sing.
Some call this the soul's longing.
Some call it your inner spring.
Indeed your heart is blossoming ~
blossoming out to contain the world.

They say birds of a feather
tend to flock together.
Have you chosen healthy friendships?

To be a good friend,
listen to the song in another's heart.
Encourage the light in her soul.
Always assure her
that her dreams are safe with you.

Seek out those who listen
to their own deep inner wisdom;
those who know the light
and who cherish other's joy.

Do not forget your True Nature.
Do not forget your Self.
Your partnership with the Sacred
will energize your days.

As the day follows night,
every winter is followed by spring.
Flowers bloom again, nectar-filled,
to sip for new energy,
peace and well being.

The garden of love is beckoning,
luring you with its fragrance,
enchanting you with its songs...
Drinking its waters, you laugh.
Breathing its air makes you dance.

Remembering you are loved,
you return to the garden again.
Looking within, you smile ~
the garden was always there.

Plant these words like seeds
in the garden of your heart:
Love is, has been,
and will always be there ~
holding you, held by you,
abundant, eternal, infinite,
without boundary, without end.

May your soul absorb
the fragrance of love.
May your heart sing out
its many songs.
May your body dance,
uplifted by its wings.
May your mind always know
expanding peaceful joy.
and through everything
you do, my love,
make honey with your life.

HONEY QUOTES

"Life is the flower for which love is the honey."
~Victor Hugo

"I have gathered my myrrh with my spice,
I have eaten my honeycomb with my honey."
~Song of Songs

"God is like the honey hive. He doesn't mind me calling him that. When you are kind, sweet, he draws you in."
~Saint Francis

The flies seek filth, the bees seek honey. I will shun the habit of the flies and follow that of the bees. I will refrain from finding faults in others and only look for the good which is in them. (Hindu vow)

End Notes

Page 19 ~ Brhadaranyaka Upanishads contain the verse,
"This Self is the Honey in all beings, and all beings are the honey in this Self."

Page 48
This passage is adapted from
Ecclesiasticus 39:13-14

Page 51
These filling mediations are adapted from several biblical references to faith being nourishment, as a stream is to a tree- found particularly in Psalms.

Page 54
These passages are inspired by
Song of Solomon 2:1-2, and 2:3-5

Page 67
These words are from the Dzogghen Tantra, "As the bee gathers nectar from all kinds of flowers, seek teachings everywhere."

Page 74
The passage,
"As the bee sips nectar without harming the flower, walk lightly in this world, taking no more than you need," has several inspirations. The first is a passage from the Dhammapada, sayings attributed to the Buddha, *"Just as the bee takes nectar and leaves without damaging the color or scent of the flowers, so should the sage act in the village."* The other inspiration is the Native American instruction to walk lightly, living with respect for the earth, all beings, and the many generations who will live here after we have gone.

Further Reading

The Song of Solomon
Ecclesiasticus
Psalms
The Dhammapada, sayings of Buddha
The Tao Te Ching, Lao Tzu
The Bhagavad Gita
Upanishads
The works of Thich Nhat Hanh
Poetry of Rumi
Poems and essays of Rabindranath Tagore

Illustration Credits

All illustrations are Japanese Prints courtesy of Dover Books.

p10~Hokusai Weeping Cherry and Finch
p16 ~Hiroshige Peonies
p22 ~ Hokusai Lilies
p28 ~ Hiroshige Double Petaled Cherry
p38~ Japanese Designs, Dover
42~ Hokusai Kingfisher w irises
46~ Japanese Designs
53 ~ Hokusai Peonies and butterfly
56~ Hokusai Poppies
60 ~ Hokusai Cranes on a Pine Tree
65,66,68,74,80 Japanese Designs

Also by Ingrid Goff-Maidoff

Simple Graces for Every Meal
Good Mother, Welcome
What Holds Us
Eternal Song
The Joy Book
The Abundance of Grace
Moonlight and Remembrance
Love
Friendship
Happiness
and many others

available through
www.TendingJoy.com

Ingrid Goff-Maidoff lives with her husband and two daughters on the island of Martha's Vineyard. She is the author of over a dozen books of poetry and inspiration, and the creator of a beautiful line of inspirational cards and gifts. Her work appears in numerous national anthologies. Visit her on the web at www.IngridGoffMaidoff.com